our GOVERNMENT

Its origins, systems and effects on people's lives

W.J. Carruthers

NELSON
CENGAGE Learning™

Australia • Brazil • Japan • Korea • Mexico • Singapore • Spain • United Kingdom • United States

Our Government
3 Edition
W J Carruthers

Publishing manager: Jenny Thomas
Text and cover deign: Cheryl Rowe
Typeset by: Cheryl Rowe
Production controller: Siew Han Ong

Any URLs contained in this publication were checked for currency during the production process. Note, however, that the publisher cannot vouch for the ongoing currency of URLs.

First published in 1994 as Our Government by New House Publishers Ltd

Acknowledgements
General Acknowledgements
Page 25: website image courtesy of Selwyn District Council;
Page 22, 26-27: photographs of parliamentary buildings courtesy of Parliament Service Collection; Page 28-29, 36-37: maps and images courtesy of Election NZ; Page 8, 12, and 47: artwork courtesy of Alan Barnett

Shutterstock images:
Cover photograph: Sam DCruz; Page 5: mountain biker courtesy of Val Thoermer, fruit picker courtesy of Marilyn Volan, skateboarder courtesy of Yuri Arcurs, office worker courtesy of AVAVA; Page 6: Dean Mitchell; Page 10: M Jackson; Page 18: school teacher and students courtesy of Matka Wariatka, toothbrush courtesy of PhotoPips; Page 24: illustration courtesy of Sylwia Nowik; Page 34: car courtesy of Konstantin Sutyagin, road courtesy of Trutta, bottle courtesy of Luminis; Page 35: Surgeons courtesy of Brasiliao, teacher courtesy of Zhu Difeng

From the author:
I would like to thank my wife, who put up with my many moods as I progressed with this endeavour.

For product information and technology assistance,
in **Australia call 1300 790 853;**
in **New Zealand call 0508 635 766**

For permission to use material from this text
or product, please email **aust.permissions@cengage.com**

National Library of New Zealand Cataloguing-in-Publication Data
Carruthers, W. J. (William J.)
Our government / W.J. Carruthers. 3rd ed.
ISBN 978-017018-223-2
Previous ed.: New House Publishers, 1998.
1. New Zealand.—Parliament—Juvenile literature. 2. National socialism—Juvenile literature. 3. New Zealand—Constitutional history—Juvenile literature. 4. New Zealand—Politics and government —Juvenile literature. [1. New Zealand.—Parliament. 2. National socialism. 3. New Zealand—Constitutional history. 4. New Zealand—Politics and government.] I. Title.
328.93—dc 22

Cengage Learning Australia
Level 7, 80 Dorcas Street
South Melbourne, Victoria Australia 3205

Cengage Learning New Zealand
Unit 4B Rosedale Office Park
331 Rosedale Road, Albany, North Shore 0632, NZ

For learning solutions, visit **cengage.com.au**

Printed in China by 1010 Printing International Limited.
1 2 3 4 5 6 7 13 12 11 10 09

Contents

Introduction 4

1 What is government? 5

2 Where did our ideas on government come from? 8

3 Was there a system of government here before Europeans came? 12

4 What important events helped develop our system of government? 16

5 How to form a coalition government 20

6 How is our system of government made up? 20

7 What is the difference between national and local government? 24

8 Where is New Zealand's Parliament located? 26

9 How do you go about voting? 29

10 How would I go about becoming an MP? 33

11 How are ideas made into laws? 36

12 From where does government get money and how does government spending impact on me? 37

13 How does our type of government affect our lives? 40

14 How do government decisions affect our lives? 42

15 What other systems of government exist? 44

16 How did the Nazi Party rise to power in Germany? 46

17 How did the Nazi Party control German society? 47

18 What happened if you opposed Nazi ideas? 50

19 Could there be a dictatorship in New Zealand? 54

Glossary of political terms 55

Introduction

By the end of this study you will be familiar with:

- what government is and what it does
- where we got our ideas on government from
- how the system we have in New Zealand works
- how the system compares with other systems
- the rights and responsibilities you have as a member of a group and as a member of your society
- the ways in which groups get and use leadership, and the results for communities and societies
- how our system of government affects our lives.

ISBN 9780170182232

unit one

What is government?

'Government' means different things to different people. To some it means to control or direct the public affairs of a nation. To others it means a group of people who make all the rules. To yet another group it means all those people in Parliament whom you blame when things aren't going well. To a fourth group, it is a system that forces you to do what you may not want to do.

Government means different things to different people

ISBN 9780170182232

You and a few friends are going to form your own club. In the planning of it you would have to consider many of the following questions.

- Who 'owns' the club?
- What privileges do people get from belonging?
- Who can belong to the club?
- Is there anything special people have to do to become members?
- Is it going to cost money to run the club? If so, how much and where is the money going to come from? Who is going to look after the cash?
- What tasks need to be done for your club to run efficiently?
- How are you going to decide who is responsible for doing these tasks?
- If they can't do the tasks, how are you going to remove them from their position?
- How do people leave the club?

Our system of social control at the national level is very much like control in your club. The only real difference is size. Your club operates at the local level (you and your friends in your own locality). The system of social control at the national level (your government) operates for the whole country. The ways in which you control your club, and your government controls your society, are similar.

For example:

1 People can be members of our society as long as they follow certain rules.
2 These rules are made by members of society.
3 By belonging to our society we receive certain privileges and benefits and we have certain responsibilities.
4 We can change the people we elect to make the rules if we think they aren't doing the job properly.
5 Electing is the name given to the process we go through when we choose someone from a group to do a specific job. You have probably elected class representatives in your own year levels at school.
6 We have special tasks that need people who are responsible for them.
7 We own our club.

Your club	Your government
Chairperson	Prime Minister
Treasurer	Minister of Finance
Secretary	Parliamentary Secretaries
Committee members	Members of Parliament

However, your club and your government are different in one big way. Because membership of your club is small, everybody can meet and talk through ideas before a decision is made. Because membership of our society is large, we elect people to go to a meeting called the Parliament. These people are our Members of Parliament (MPs) and they are meant to represent their ideas with which we agree. That is why we voted for them.

ISBN 9780170182232

The place where government meets to do its job is called Parliament. It is in Wellington. Our government is made up of all those Members of Parliament who belong to the political party that got the most people elected. It could also be made up of those parties that, joined together, had the most people elected.

All the other Members of Parliament are said to be the Opposition. They oppose and argue against the government. They try to get people to see that there may be other ways of doing things.

Activities

1 Trace Resource 2 and match people with what they think government is from Resource 1.

2 Complete the following sentence. 'I think government is ...'

3 Working in small groups use Resource 3 to develop a set of rules for a club of your choice. Ideas could come from any sports activity, cultural activity or leisure activity. Let your imagination soar!
Your teacher may allow you to make wall charts under such headings as 'Rules of the ... Club'. If so, make sure you have a copy in your notes.

4 Using Resource 4 draw a star diagram around the theme 'Similarities between a club and a government'. Make your diagram at least half a page in size.

5 Using the Net:
Find out where the word 'Parliament' comes from, what different names are used for it in some other countries, and what a good definition for it is.

When using the internet make sure you reference the websites you visit. Do the same for any books or published material you use.

Where did our ideas on government come from?

The origins of democracy

New Zealand has a democratic system of government. This means we can describe New Zealand as being a democracy. Democracy is not the only system of government at work in the world and we will be studying other systems.

The word 'democracy' comes from the Ancient Greek word 'demos' meaning people and 'kratos' meaning to rule. Our original ideas about democracy came from a system of social control developed in Ancient Greece. The people of Athens, an important place in Ancient Greece, had a say in how they were governed. This was the first formal democracy recorded. It lasted only 40 years, from 469 BC to 429 BC. This period is sometimes referred to as the Golden Age of Greek culture. Ancient Greek power lasted from 550 BC to 130 BC.

Some of these democratic ideas were later adopted by the next major power to develop around the Mediterranean Sea. This was the Roman Empire. The Romans had Senates where Senators met to discuss the day-to-day running of the Empire. However, senators could only advise the Roman emperor. It was the emperor who made the decisions. The idea of one person representing a large group of people came from this period. As well, many of our ideas about law and peoples' rights under the law were developed. The Roman Empire spanned 600 years from 130 BC to 470 AD.

Greek city states:

- A city state comprised of the city and the immediate land around it.
- Athens and Sparta were known as city states.
- Athens had a population of around 20,000 people.
- To enable a system of direct government by citizens to work you have to have a small state and limit the numbers who could be called citizens.
- The English word 'idiot' comes from the Greek word that means a private citizen. A private citizen was one who only looked after his own affairs and didn't bother with the affairs of the city.
- Sparta's population was approximately 1,500-2,000 citizens plus many thousands of slaves. At one time, citizens could legally kill slaves.
- Farmers on land surrounding the city provided food for the city people.
- Sparta had a different form of government to Athens. It was known for its more military-type government.
- Athens and Sparta were bitter enemies and rivals.

ISBN 9780170182232

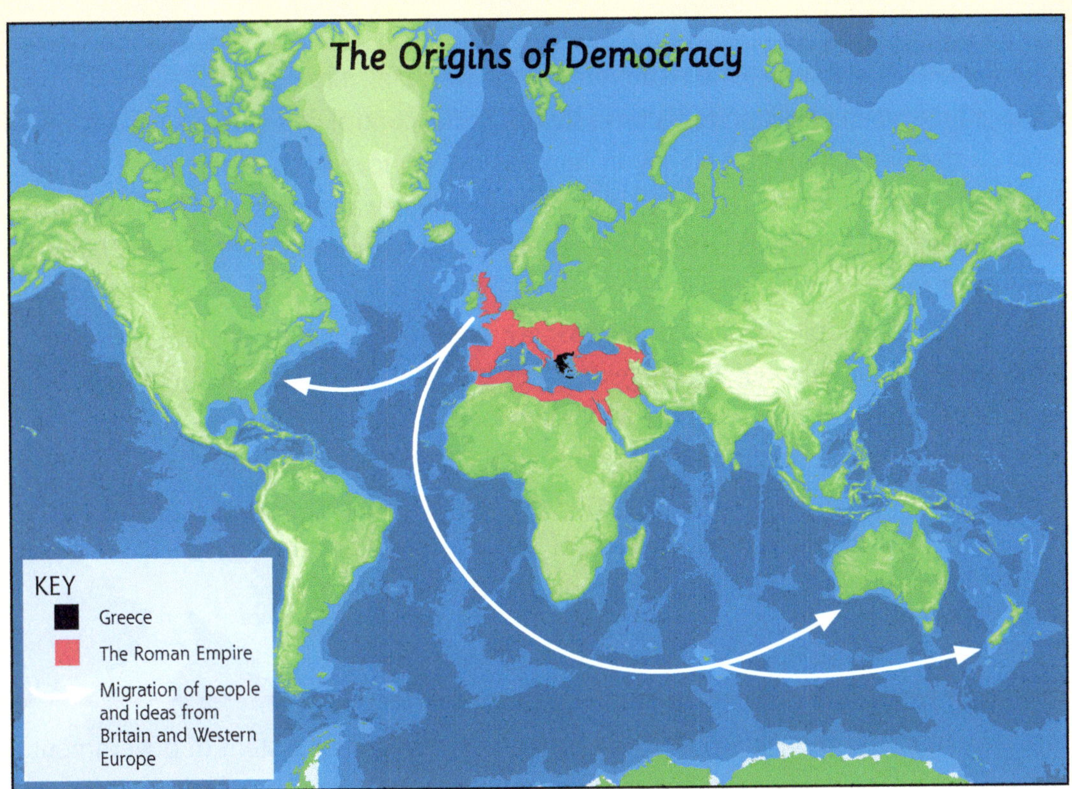

Comparison of Athens and Sparta

Function	Athens	Sparta
To be a citizen	Male. Over 30. Of Athenian parents.	Male or female. Over 30. Descendant from original inhabitants of the city.
Making decisions	Made by the assembly.	Made by the kings.
Who belonged to the decision-making group	All citizens.	Two kings, a group of officials (ephors) and a committee of 28 elders (over 60) elected for life.
Where decisions were made	In an area of the marketplace called the Agora.	In the Royal court.
Who ran the day-to-day affairs of the city	A council of 500 citizens elected for a 1 year term.	The Royal court.
Choice of leaders	Voted for by the citizens.	Descendants of the kings.
Jobs available	Could choose what job they liked.	Only males allowed to be soldiers.
Formal education	Boys only – studied music, debating, reading and writing.	Boys and girls received training in physical fitness, reading, writing, music and dance. Boys received further intensive weapons training.
Female dress and bearing	Heavy, concealing clothing. Rarely seen outside the house.	Girls wore short dresses. Women went where they pleased.
Status of women	Inferior to men, owned no property.	Controlled their own property. Laws of divorce the same for men and women.

ISBN 9780170182232

With the fall of the Roman Empire this area of the world fell into a period called 'The Dark Ages'. It was a time when new kingdoms were set up. Social control was with a king and his advisors. Most of the population had no say in how they were governed. Knowledge about how the Athenians and the Romans used to govern themselves was almost lost. However, monks in monasteries could study in safety. They preserved the knowledge of ancient languages and systems of social control.

By 1500 AD people began to successfully question many of the basic values of the previous 1,000 years. This period is known as the Renaissance (re-birth). Art, sculpture and poetry became popular. Sailors from Western Europe started to explore the world. People re-discovered science. Knowledge held in the monasteries poured out. Part of that knowledge was the democratic system of social control practised in ancient Athens and the legal systems developed by Ancient Rome.

Over the next 350 years many of the kingdoms changed their system of government. Instead of the king having total control, people were elected to represent areas of the kingdom. Britain in particular had evolved a system of elected representation. The transfer of power took time and was not always peaceful. This is the time of the English Civil War (1642-58), the American War of Independence (1775-81) and the French Revolution (1789).

At the end of this period New Zealand was being re-settled by its second wave of immigrants. These were the British and people from West Europe who arrived after the signing of the Treaty of Waitangi in 1840. They brought with them the system of government which had developed in their homelands. This system, modified many times, is the one we have today. People often refer to it as the Westminster System after the site of the British Houses of Parliament.

Comparisons between the Ancient Athenian system of government and New Zealand's system of government

	Ancient Athens	New Zealand
Who can have a say	You have to be male, over 30 and of Athenian parents.	Any person over 18 can vote, so long as they are not serving a prison sentence.
Attendance at the Assembly	Anyone who is a citizen can attend the Assembly.	Only those people who are elected by the voters can attend Parliament. (Parliament is our Assembly.)
Time of service	Once a month.	People are elected for three years as a full-time job.
Responsibility for day-to-day running	A Council of 500 people who are chosen by lot and can serve only one year.	We have a civil service (Government Departments) which are full-time employed workers.
Choice of leaders	Decided by those attending the Assembly.	Chosen by the party that wins the election.

 ISBN 9780170182232

For a country to have a full democracy, women have to have the same voting rights as men. This was not always the case in places like Britain and New Zealand. The term 'women's suffrage' was used to describe the movement that aimed to get women the vote. Suffrage is another word for 'vote'. Women who worked to get Parliament to pass a law giving them the vote were called suffragettes. Opponents of women's suffrage used arguments such as a woman's place was in the home, and if women got the vote they would talk politics instead of getting dinner. People in favour of women's suffrage said the female brain was equal to that of the male and females had just as much as males to contribute to society and government. In 1893 Parliament in New Zealand passed a law giving women the vote. New Zealand was the first Parliament in the world to do this. Other Parliaments such as the British and Australian Parliaments did so later.

Activities

1 Draw a time line to show the main events mentioned in this unit.
Use a scale of 1cm = 100 years and make your line 25cm long. This represents 2,500 years. Start your line at 500 BC and end it at 2000 AD.
Illustrate your time line with drawings from the periods mentioned so you can 'read' your time line without referring to words.

Time Line

500 BC | 0 | 500 AD | 1000 AD | 1500 AD | 2000 AD

2 Write a series of paragraphs outlining ways in which the Athenian system of government has influenced our system of government. Work in small groups. Make sure you talk about what you are going to write before your group puts a finished copy together.

3 Using the Net:
Choose one or more of the following research activities:

- Find out more about life in Sparta and Athens. Decide which one you would have preferred to be a citizen of and explain why.
- Prepare a project on why women were not allowed to have a say in running many societies in the past. Include the role of New Zealand women in making this country's Parliament the first Parliament in modern history to give women the right to vote.
- Describe how New Zealand became the first Parliament in modern history to give women the vote.

When using the internet make sure you reference the websites you visit. Do the same for any books or published material you use.

ISBN 9780170182232

Was there a system of government here before Europeans came?

The first wave of immigrants to arrive in Aotearoa developed tribal (iwi) structures. Each of the main tribal groups can trace the ancestral landing place where their original canoe came ashore – this was their part of New Zealand.

Canoe landfalls of some of the major tribal groups

Canoe	Landfall	Main Tribal Group	Location
Mamari	Hokianga Harbour	Ngapuhi	North Hokianga, Whangaroa.
Ngatokimatawhaorua	Hokianga Harbour	Ngapuhi	Hokianga, Bay of Islands.
Mahuhu	Kaipara Harbour	Ngati Whatua	North Auckland Area.
Tainui	Kawhia Harbour	Waikato	Mokau (West Coast) in a sweeping curve to Waihi on the east coast. All land between this line and Auckland.
Te Arawa	Maketu	Te Arawa	Bay of Plenty Coast to central North Island.
Tokomaru	Mohakatino River	Ngati Tama	North and Central Taranaki.
Aotea	Aotea Harbour	Ngati Ruanui	South Taranaki and Wanganui.
Horouta	Waiapu River	Ngati Porou	East Coast (north of Poverty Bay).
Matatua	Whakatane	Ngati Awa	Eastern Bay of Plenty (inland to Waikaremoana).
Takitimu	Waiau River	Ngati Kahungunu Ngai Tahu	Poverty Bay to Wellington, South Island.

When they first arrived these ancestors of today's New Zealand Maori had plenty of room to move. They roamed over the land, exploring, hunting and exchanging gifts such as greenstone and preserved birds.

ISBN 9780170182232

By 1500 AD the population had grown to a point where competition for the better areas was fierce. Small groups of related hapu (extended family) started to join together for protection and to help each other in food production. By this stage most of the early New Zealanders had a knowledge of the shape and landscape of New Zealand. There was no need, however, to join other iwi in the sense of a nation. Occasionally iwi allied themselves together for protection from raids from other iwi groups. There was never an alliance of all the iwi under one organisation.

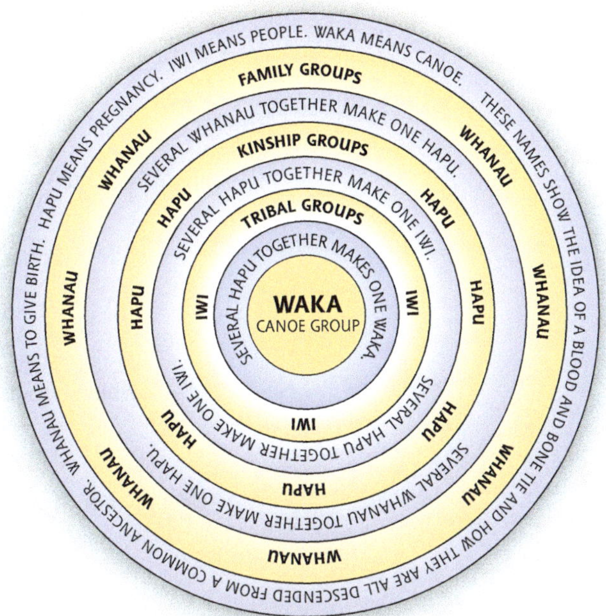

At the time of the signing of the Treaty of Waitangi each iwi governed its own tribal area. The most powerful chief was referred to as the paramount chief of the iwi.

Common tribal members could debate issues on their whanau's marae. Their chief or head of the whanau could then take undecided issues at the whanau level to the hapu marae. After further debate decisions were either made or the issue was brought to the paramount chief's marae for his advice.

Even though there was no idea of a government for all Maori tribes, many Maori chiefs signed a Declaration of Independence in 1835. This suggests that there was some idea of iwi having things in common.

resource 3

Why was this system replaced by a European style of government?

- This system was tribal and based on distinct tribal areas.
- Maori did not think of New Zealand as one nation.
- The huge numbers of people making up the second wave of immigrants thought of New Zealand as one place and wanted one national government system.
- Because New Zealand became a colony of Great Britain, a system of government similar to Britain's was established.
- The new immigrants had no tribal relationships.

Activities

1 Trace a map of New Zealand. Using Resource 1 and the internet, place arrows identifying original iwi (tribal) areas. Add the canoes to your arrows.

 ISBN 9780170182232

2 Maori developed iwi structures. Copy and complete this flow diagram to illustrate how this iwi was organised.

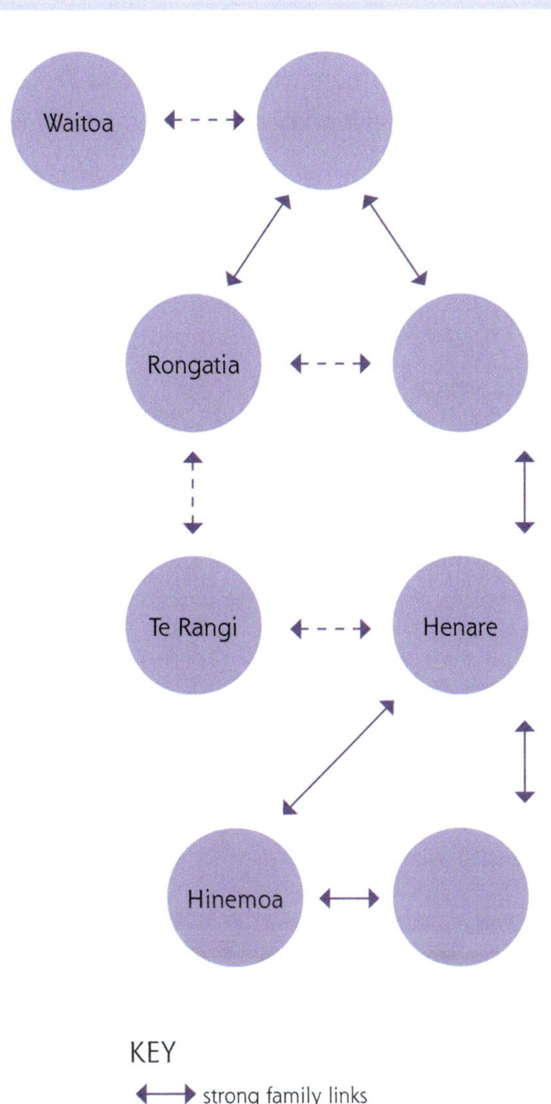

Rata	A member of Henare's whanau
Te Rangi	Henare's cousin
Wiremu	Rata's hapu chief
Hinemoa	Rata's younger sister
Rongatia	Chief of a hapu who is related through marriage to Te Rangi's wife's sister.
Te Whero	Chief of Wiremu's iwi
Waitoa	Tohunga and advisor to Te Whero
Henare	Whanau chief

KEY

⟷ strong family links

⇠⇢ less strong family links

3 Using the Net:

Choose one or more of the following research activities.

- Prepare a project on the main points in the history of peoples from one of the canoes in Resource 1.
- Prepare a project on the 1835 Declaration of Independence. Why did Maori of the time feel they needed to make this declaration, what did it involve and what happened to it after the Treaty of Waitangi was signed? Put your project notes over a copy of their flag. A good web site to visit is www.archives.govt.nz

When using the internet make sure you reference the websites you visit. Do the same for any books or published material you use.

ISBN 9780170182232

What important events helped develop our system of government

Even though immigrants from Britain brought their ideas on government with them to New Zealand, there were many official events that had to happen before New Zealand became a democracy with its own government.

1840	Treaty of Waitangi made New Zealand a colony of Britain. It was governed from the British Colonial Office in London.
1852	The Constitution Act introduced a Parliament to New Zealand.
1853	The first 37 men were elected to Parliament. The only people who could vote at this time were property-owning European men.
1865	Parliament moved from Auckland to Wellington.
1867	Separate Maori seats in Parliament were set up.
1870	Secret voting was introduced. This meant nobody could see for whom other people voted.
1879	All men over 21 years old were allowed to vote.
1893	All women over 21 years old were allowed to vote.
1907	New Zealand stopped being a colony and became a self-governing Dominion. Our laws still had to be acceptable to Britain.
1947	New Zealand became fully independent and was a sovereign state in its own right.

(CAM 1) NEWSREADER (AUTOCUE)

In 1993 New Zealand voters ditched the First-Past-The-Post political system in favour of MMP. MMP stands for Mixed Member Proportional representation. In the 2008 election night results the original 120 seats were expanded to 122.

In a recent election 64 MPs were elected and 56 were appointed from party lists. The party list is the list of people, in order of importance, the party wants to have in Parliament. Who goes into Parliament off the party list depends on how many seats the party got from the party vote and how many electorate MPs they have. This mix can vary because the numbers and borders of the electorates are reviewed after every election. Under MMP every voter has two votes. The first vote is for the party the voter most wants to see in Parliament. The second vote is for the local candidate the voter wants to be the Electorate MP. The first vote is used to calculate how many seats in Parliament each party may have.

In this way the total number of Members of Parliament a party has will generally reflect its share of the total vote. Smaller parties are represented in Parliament under the MMP system. Therefore coalitions, parties joining together, or agreements between parties are often needed to form governments.

 ISBN 9780170182232

Activities

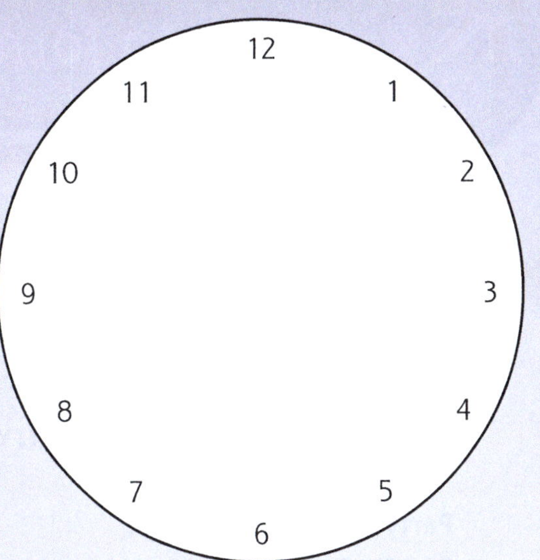

1 Draw a large clock face in your notes.
- Where the 12 would be write 1840.
- Continue around the clock in groups of 10 years. 1 would become 1850, 2 would become 1860 and so on.
- Mark on your clock face the important events listed in Resource 1.
- Colour-code your clock face.
- Entitle your clock face 'The Time to Independence'.
- Under your clock face add:
  - In 1974 all people 18 and over can vote.
  - In 1993 New Zealand adopted Mixed Member Proportional Representation (MMP) voting.

2 An MMP Election Result
Consider Resource 2 and then, on an enlarged copy of the seating plan of the 122 seat House of Representatives, colour in the block of seats won by each of the parties in the 2008 Election. For each party write on the seats 'E' for 'Elected' seats or 'L' for 'List' seats. You will find a blank diagram at www.newhouse.co.nz/title/0170182231/2484

Party	% of vote	Seats	Elected	List
National	45.9	59	39	20
Labour	33.8	43	24	19
Green	6.5	8	0	8
Act	3.7	5	1	4
Maori	2.3	5	5	0
United Future	0.9	1	1	0
Progressive	0.9	1	1	0

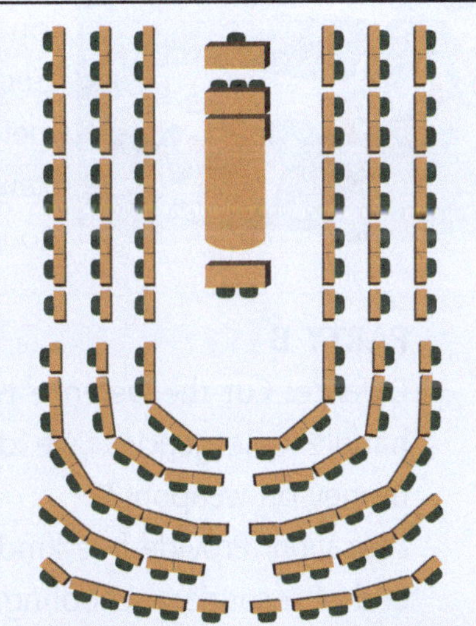

3 Using the Net:
Research the differences between First-Past-The-Post and MMP.

When using the internet make sure you reference the websites you visit. Do the same for any books or published material you use.

ISBN 9780170182232

How to form a coalition government

resource 1

In a recent election no one party gained a majority of the seats so the parties are going to have to join together in order to get a majority of more than 62 seats.
Number of seats gained by each party in the122 seat Parliament:

PARTY A – 40 PARTY B – 19 PARTY C – 42 PARTY D – 21

Party Policy Statements:

PARTY A

Defence: A strong Defence Force is needed. We need to spend more on armaments to ensure our armed forces are fully trained on modern equipment so that they are in minimum danger when sent into conflict.

Education: We will develop user choice where people are given vouchers to pay the school of their choice.

Agriculture: We will reintroduce monetary assistance to farmers so that they can remain financial and therefore stay in production.

Health: Hospitals will be free for all but doctors' fees will be charged on all visits.

Social Welfare: People will need to work on special tasks before they get any benefits.

Law and Order: We are going to train 500 more police. We will get tough on criminals.

PARTY B

Defence: Cut the Defence Force. Establish a Civil Defence Force to handle emergencies. We don't have any enemies so why spend money on weapons?

Education: Provide free kindergartens and free dental health to the end of secondary schooling.

Agriculture: Control the exchange rate so that our farmers can earn a decent living off the land.

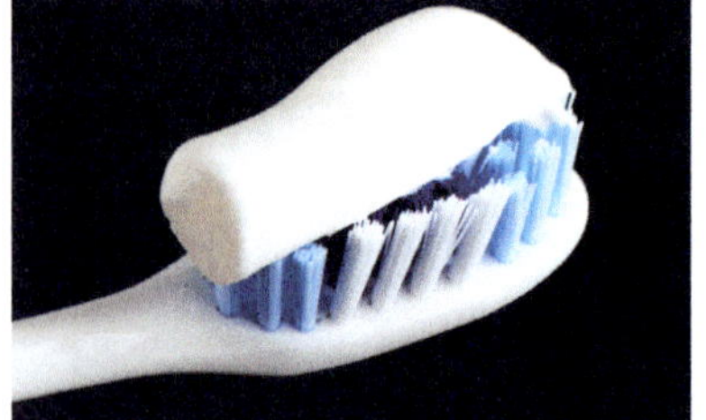

Health: People should contribute to their own health care by having compulsory health insurance.

Social Welfare: A special tax will be imposed to ensure that there is enough money to support all those who need it.

Law and Order: Make parents more accountable for their children. Most crime is committed by under 24 year olds.

 ISBN 9780170182232

PARTY C

Defence: Cut the Defence Force to 'Coastguard' status and use our navy to protect fisheries resources.

Education: Provide tax cuts so that people can pay school fees which will be compulsory.

Agriculture: Farmers should be exposed to market forces. If they cannot make a go of it they should sell up.

Health: Doctors visits for under 13 year olds are free. However, free hospital access will be measured against the assets of the patient.

Social Welfare: Those on a benefit will have to attend training courses to improve their employment chances.

Law and Order: Encourage the private security industry with financial grants to take over much of the fulltime police force's non-criminal work.

PARTY D

Defence: Maintain our armed forces at their current strength so that we can successfully help United Nations peace-keeping operations.

Education: Ensure that all teachers are paid on the same scale regardless of where in the education system they teach.

Agriculture: Provide no direct assistance. Instead provide more research funds to improve the competitive nature of our farming industry.

Health: We should have a special tax that goes to fund our health system so that all people can access the health services they need.

Social Welfare: The community, not the government, is responsible for ensuring as few people as possible are on a benefit. We will give some funding to help those communities develop schemes.

Law and Order: We will build another maximum security prison to help clear the streets of criminals.

Activities

1 Examine Resource 1. Study the policy statements of each party under the six key policy areas. Group the parties according to those that have similar policies.
   - How many times does the same combination of parties occur?
   - In what policy areas do these combinations occur?

Divide into groups of 4 so that each member of the group represents a different political party: A, B, C or D.
   - Debate with your group and agree on which parties are going to join together to form a coalition government.
   - Write down what your coalition government is going to do in the six policy areas. You must agree on what you are going to do before you write it down.
   - Each group reports back on what arrangements they came to.

When using the internet make sure you reference the websites you visit. Do the same for any books or published material you use.

ISBN 9780170182232

How is our system of government made up?

There are four main parts to our system of government:

1 **Executive Council:** this group runs the country by making the day-to-day decisions which the Civil Service (often called the Public Service) carries out. It is also referred to as Cabinet and is made up of the Prime Minister and other members of her/his party who have special areas of society to look after. These other members are referred to as Ministers. For example, the Minister of Education.
2 **The Legislative:** the main body of Parliament that makes the laws.
3 **The Judiciary:** these are the judges and law courts of our land that enforce and interpret the law.
4 **The Governor-General:** the Queen's representative because the Queen, as New Zealand's Head of State, is part of our Government but obviously cannot physically be in New Zealand.

The Executive and Legislative are made up of Members of Parliament, the people we vote for, while the judiciary are appointed.

All of these parts are kept separate so that no one part of the government can gain too much power.

The Governor-General represents the Queen or King. He or she is a symbol of national unity and leadership. As such the Governor-General is separate from the 'business' of government. He or she has no part in the daily activities of the House of Representatives but rather has roles away from government.

The Governor-General:

- Receives the writ to dissolve Parliament before a general election.
- Requests the leader of the party with the most parliamentary support to form a new government after a general election.
- Assents to bills so that they become Acts of Parliament.
- Opens Parliament by giving a speech from the throne. This speech sets out what the Government is going to do in the next term of Parliament.
- Swears in the government Ministers.
- The Governor-General gives honours to people, welcomes Heads of State from other countries, receives credentials from foreign diplomats.
- Acts as patron of many charitable, service, sporting and cultural organisations.
- Does ceremonial jobs such as opening important new buildings, delivering speeches to open conferences and launching special appeals.

ISBN 9780170182232

What does Parliament do?

1 Parliament is the group of people from which a government is selected and which provides an opposition group to those in government.
2 Parliament approves any spending the government wants to do (the Budget). The money Government gets to spend comes from people paying their income taxes and various charges such as Road User Charges, GST, petrol levies, customs duties.
3 Parliament is the place where government ideas can be criticised and other ideas put forward.
4 Parliament is the place where ordinary people can have their ideas voiced through their Member of Parliament (MP).
5 Parliament is where laws are argued about and decided upon for the benefit of the nation.
6 Parliament is where the Governor-General gives the 'Royal Assent' or approval to ideas before they are called laws.

Being an MP

Daily Schedule

6.00 am	Get up and prepare for work.
7.00 am	Arrive at Parliament and answer correspondence.
7.45 am	Breakfast at desk while meeting with other MPs and helping electorate members.
8.30 am	Attend a management meeting to discuss the day's organisation.
9.00 am	Attend Law and Order Select Committee meeting.
10.00 am	Attend the party meeting called 'caucus' where all the party MPs discuss policy issues.
1.00 pm	Lunch break to discuss who is going to do what in the House (the debating chamber).
2.00 pm	Go to the House (with other MPs) where the parliamentary programme for the day is debated.
5.30 pm	Dinner break. Also used to attend official dinners and meetings.
7.30 pm	House resumes for the evening.
10.30 pm	The House rises for the evening. Work on correspondence helping electorate members.
11.00 pm	Home for a shower and sleep.

ISBN 9780170182232

Weekly schedule

Sunday	Spend time with the family in the electorate.
Monday	Meet people in the electorate who need help. Prepare to go to Wellington.
Tuesday	Return to Wellington to be at Parliament by 9.00am
Wednesday	Daily Schedule.
Thursday	Daily Schedule.
Friday	Daily Schedule. Prepare to return to the electorate.
Saturday	Meet people in the electorate who need help.

For an idea to become law it must be brought before Parliament three times.

1 It is read in Parliament. From there it goes to a committee made up of members of Parliament who specialise in the field with which the idea is concerned. This is called a 'Select Committee'. The committee listens to people's views on the idea (submissions). The committee then debates the idea and its possible effects on New Zealand. This is where a lot of input and changes to the original idea take place. The idea is adjusted to make it more acceptable to other members of Parliament. Most of the work in developing an idea into a law is done at Select Committee stage. The Select Committee is the powerhouse of government.

2 & 3 The second and third times an idea is returned to Parliament allows more members of Parliament to have their say.

How ideas become laws is more fully explored in Unit 10.

Select Committees – the powerhouse of government

Select committees work on behalf of the House. Once a bill is referred to a select committee they have approximately 6 months to carefully look at the bill and prepare a report for the House. Select committees will usually ask for public submissions and then hold public hearings to listen to people present some of the submissions. It is their job to decide what changes, if any, should be made to the bill and report their conclusions back to the House.

 ISBN 9780170182232

Activities

1 Design a simple star diagram around the central idea 'Parts that make up our government'.

2 Imagine you are the MP for your electorate. Write up your diary for seven days describing a typical week in Wellington.

3 You are a member of a Defence Review Select Committee. A Bill has been introduced into Parliament re-establishing the Royal New Zealand Airforce's combat strike wing. Your committee's task is to hear all the submissions on this matter and bring the Bill back into Parliament for its second reading. Below are some of the many submissions you have heard.

1 The government should never have done away with our strike wing in the first place. It was a very bad mistake.
2 We don't need fighter aircraft – who do they think they are going to shoot down?
3 We have to have a combat wing to provide air cover when our army is called on for peace-keeping duties. We had to rely on the Australians for cover when we landed in East Timor – what an embarrassment!
4 Fighter aircraft are a waste of time and money. Our scarce resources are better spent on more helicopters and C-130 Hercules cargo planes.
5 New Zealand has to contribute to its own defence. If we can't be seen to be helping ourselves why should any other nation bother to help us when we need it?
6 Our existing strike wing was so obsolete – we were flying 30 year old jets! We need to totally re-equip with F-15s to have any credibility with our allies.
7 Having a strike wing is only pandering to those who want more expensive toys.
8 The Americans are phasing out their F-15s in readiness for the introduction of the F/A 22 Raptor. We could pick up an F-15 squadron at a bargain price.
9 All our fighter pilots are now flying with the RAF and the Australian Airforce. It will take four years to get a pool of skilled pilots even if we could get the instructors.
10 Why don't we go straight to UAV (Unmanned Aerial Vehicles)? The Americans have already used them to fire missiles at ground targets. With advances in GPS and Ground Control technologies we could have an unmanned combat strike wing.
11 During the Second World War we lost large numbers of New Zealand men in Greece and Crete because we relied on other nations to supply air cover. Air cover didn't happen then and there is no reason to believe we can guarantee air cover now. We must learn from our own history.
12 We have taken the first step in refusing to waste money on war equipment. Let the rest of the world applaud us and follow our example. Then, perhaps, there will be a true world peace.

Decide what you are going to recommend to Parliament. List the arguments you would use in support of your position.

4 Using the Net:
Gather a list of current government Ministers and their portfolios (jobs they do in Parliament), such as Minister of Education.

When using the internet make sure you reference the websites you visit. Do the same for any books or published material you use.

ISBN 9780170182232

What is the difference between national and local government?

Imagine if members of government had to concern themselves with where to put the local rubbish dump or how to control stray dogs in the local park. They would not have enough time to attend to those matters that affected the nation as a whole.

To overcome this, a system of local government has been developed. Local authorities and councils deal with issues that are important to local people.

We choose members of our local government in the same way as we choose members of our national government. These elections are called Local Body elections.

The national government sets guidelines and advises local governments on how to do things and what is required by law. The national government also provides some money. However, most of the local government money comes from rates paid by the local property owners.

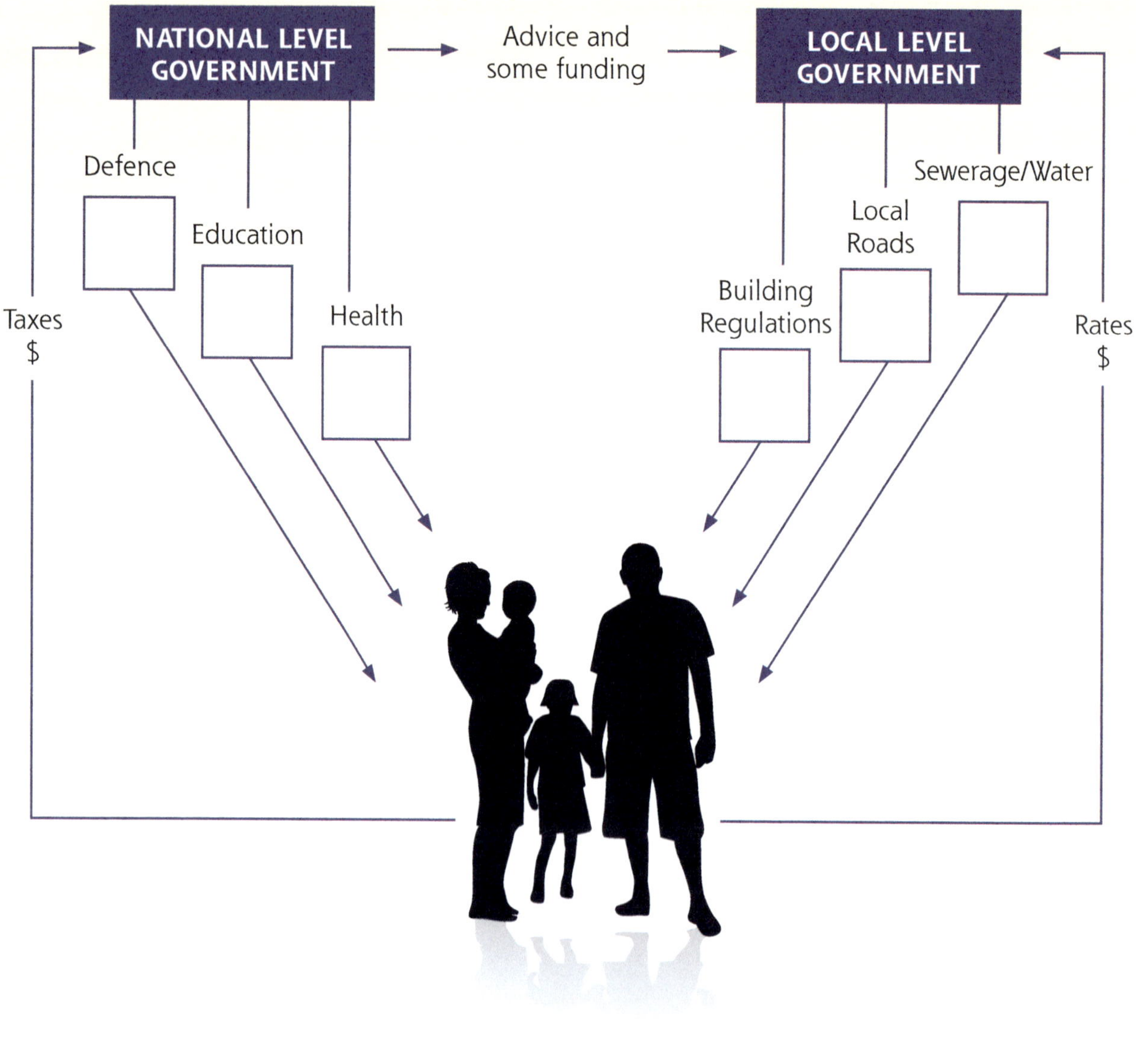

NATIONAL LEVEL GOVERNMENT → Advice and some funding → LOCAL LEVEL GOVERNMENT

Defence

Education

Health

Building Regulations

Local Roads

Sewerage/Water

Taxes $

Rates $

ISBN 9780170182232

Activities

1 Copy the diagram from Resource 1.
Place the following events in the correct empty boxes on the diagram – just put the key words (underlined) in the boxes
- Part of your school burns down and relocatable classrooms arrive.
- RNZAF helicopters air-drop hay to starving sheep caught in a snow storm.
- A new children's ward is built at your nearest hospital.
- Your dad had to get a permit before he could add the extra room to your house.
- A new bridge is built at the end of your road to replace the one washed out last winter.
- The burst water pipe outside your home is repaired.

2 Take a close look at Resource 2 and use the information you find to prepare a brochure on what services this council provides. Alternatively access your own council's web sites or visit their offices and prepare a brochure on it.

3 Using the Net:
Choose one or more of the following research activities.
- Contact your local council and identify who the elected representatives are and what they are responsible for. Produce a chart of your results.
- Research the stages you would have to go through if you wanted your local council to develop a facility for teenagers in your locality. Use your imagination as to what it could be.

When using the internet make sure you reference the websites you visit. Do the same for any books or published material you use.

ISBN 9780170182232

Where is New Zealand's Parliament located?

New Zealand's first Parliament sat in Auckland on 24 May 1854. Many of the members of Parliament had to sail to Auckland from other regions of the country. For some this was a journey of up to two months. People were already questioning the sense of having Parliament so far in the north of the country. They were suggesting it move to a more central location. Many years of argument followed.

It took a group of independent Australian commissioners to make the final decision. In 1865 Parliament moved to Wellington where it has stayed since.

Today if you visit Wellington you will find four main buildings that make up the place we call 'Parliament'.

1 Parliament House

This is at the centre of Parliament. Its architecture is more old-fashioned. In front of it is a large paved area. This is used as a parade ground for a 100-person Guard. Chauffeurs drop important people off here. It is the place where protesters tend to gather. It is also the building that often forms the backdrop for TV items about government activities.

Inside the building is the heart of Parliament. This is the Chamber. People often refer to it as the Debating Chamber. This is where the House of Representatives meets to debate bills and consider parliamentary business. Above, and surrounding the Chamber, is the gallery. This is where the public and media can sit and listen to the debates.

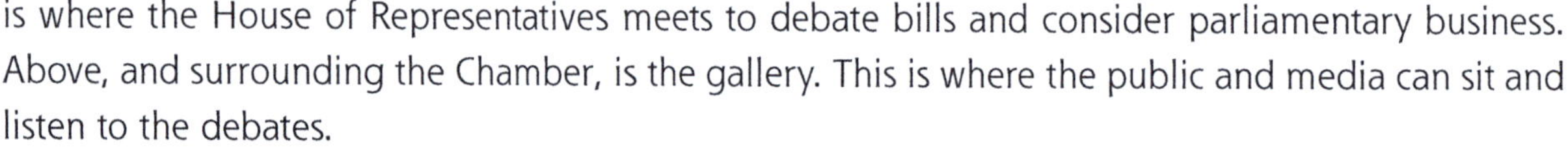

Parliament House also has the Maori Affairs committee room and the Pacific room used for Select Committee hearings.

Right through Parliament House, from front to rear, runs the Galleria. This is a 4-storey high, 30-metre long, 5-metre wide thoroughfare. On the first floor is the 27 metre long Grand Hall.

A number of Member of Parliament's offices with their support staff are also located in the wings of Parliament House.

2 The Executive Wing

Referred to as the 'Beehive' this building houses the offices of the Prime Minister and Cabinet Ministers. It also houses the Cabinet room where the Cabinet meets. It is on the southeast side of Parliament House.

It has the Banquet Hall which can seat up to 300 people for state banquets. There are also several function rooms, a theatrette,

ISBN 9780170182232

swimming pool, TV studios and Bellamy's restaurant. These are available to all MPs.

In the basement of the Executive Wing is the National Crisis Management Centre. This is the Government's command centre when there is a major emergency or security threat.

3 Bowen House

This is a modern 22-storey building across Bowen Street from the Beehive. It is joined to the Beehive by an underground passage. This building provides office space for many MPs and parliamentary support teams. Also in this building are additional Select Committee rooms, function areas for formal and informal gatherings, conference and meeting rooms.

4 Parliamentary Library

This is on the northwest side of Parliament House. Thomas Turnbull designed it in the 1880s and 90s. It used to be called the General Assembly Library. It has research services for MPs. It also has public reading rooms. This is where the Parliamentary Information Service is located.

Activities

1 Locate a street map of the Parliamentary area (check out www.wises.co.nz as a start). Draw in the main buildings in this unit. Add the High Court and the Court of Appeal (across the road on the north side of Molesworth St.).

2 Parliament is all about debating an issue. Carefully think about the idea ...

That Auckland, with over 25% of New Zealand's population, should be the seat of Government.

Choose which side you believe in and write a persuasive essay explaining why people should agree with you. Give reasons for your arguments.

3 Using the Net:

Choose one or more of the following research activities.

- Find out how the Parliament Buildings have been built to withstand earthquakes given that they are constructed on a fault line.
- Find out how the Beehive got its name.

When using the internet make sure you reference the websites you visit. Do the same for any books or published material you use.

ISBN 9780170182232

How do you go about voting?

We have discovered that one of the things we value is the idea that everyone over 18-years-old should have a say in how they are governed. Unlike Ancient Athens we can't all go to the Agora and debate the current issues. Instead, we have a system whereby we elect people, whose ideas we like, to represent us at a gathering called Parliament located in Wellington. Voting is the process by which we can have our say in who represents us.

An electorate is a geographic area represented by a Member of Parliament. People living in that particular area vote to see who will be their representative. Boundary-makers, who decide boundaries for electorates, make sure all electorates have roughly the same number of people living in them. This is why some electorates look bigger or smaller than others on a map.

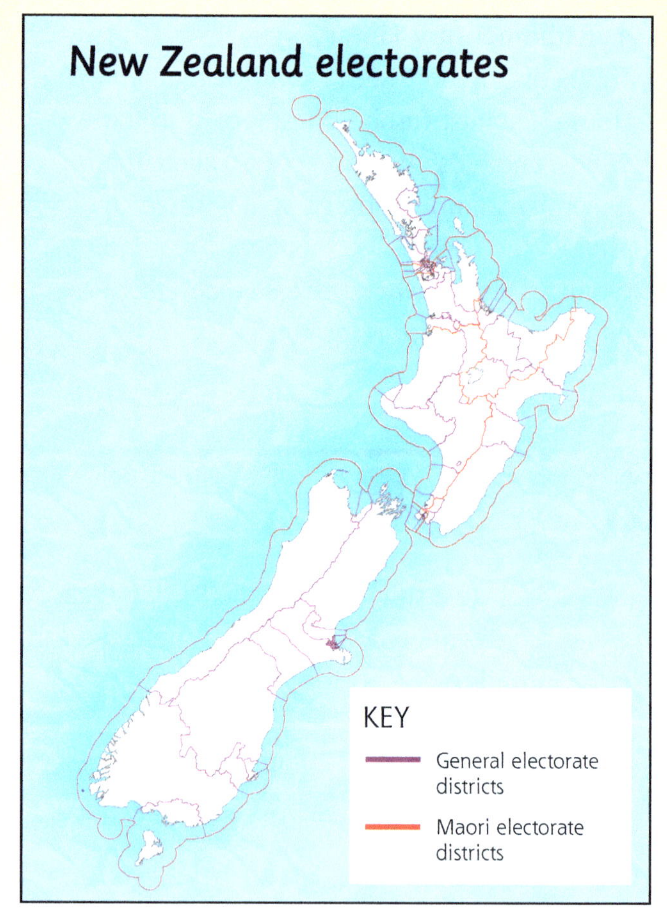

Steps involved in casting a vote:

Step 1 Make sure you are eligible to vote:

a Are you 18 years or older?
b Have you lived in the electorate continuously for 3 months?
c Have you lived in New Zealand continuously for 1 year or more?
d Are you a New Zealand citizen or permanent resident?

ISBN 9780170182232

Step 2 Make sure you register on the electoral roll.

Step 3 On election day do the following things:

a Go to a polling booth between 9am-7pm. Polling booths are often in schools or church halls.

b On entering the booth report to the Polling Officer.

c The Polling Officer will cross your name off the electoral roll and give you a numbered ballot paper.

d With your ballot paper go to the voting screens.

e When you are behind the screens nobody can see how you vote. Here you tick the ballot paper for the person who you want to vote for and also tick the Party you want to vote for.

f Fold your ballot paper, and carry it to the ballot box which is in front of the Polling Officer.

g Place your folded ballot paper in the ballot box and leave the polling booth.

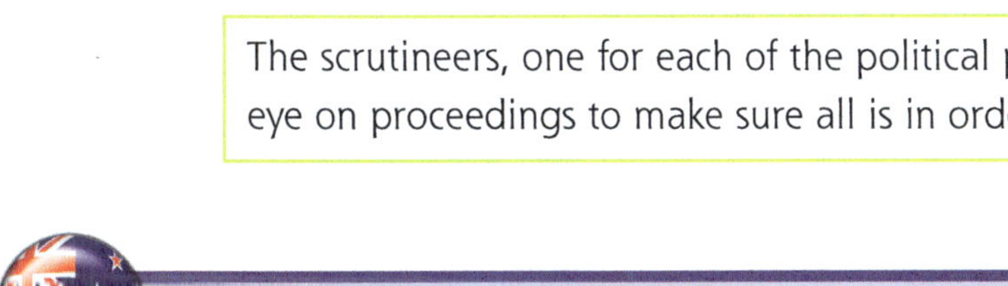
The scrutineers, one for each of the political parties, keep an eye on proceedings to make sure all is in order.

Activities

1 Give the name of the electorate you are in and explain the steps you would take to make sure your vote got counted.

2 Using the Net:
Choose one or more of the following research activities.

- Produce a list of web sites that have information about voting, government and Parliament in New Zealand. A good place to start is www.elections.org.nz

- Find out what happens after you have put your voting paper in the ballot box. How are the votes collected? Where are they counted? Who counts them? Do these people receive any training? Where are the voting papers kept in case a re-count is required? What happens to your voting paper after the election is all over?

When using the internet make sure you reference the websites you visit. Do the same for any books or published material you use.

ISBN 9780170182232

unit ten

How would I go about becoming an MP?

So you want to be a Member of Parliament and represent your electorate? As you learnt in Unit 9 any person in New Zealand who is allowed to vote is eligible to stand as a candidate for Parliament. There are some steps you have to go through.

resource 1

Steps to go through to get into Parliament

1 Decide if you want to join a political party that has similar ideas to you or if you are going to be an independent candidate. An independent candidate does not belong to any party.

2 Let's assume you are going to do what the majority of the would-be members of Parliament do and join a political party. Your next step is to convince the party that you would be a good candidate and gain selection to stand in an electorate. To gain selection you have to be chosen as the best candidate for the party by the members of the political party in that area. If there is more than one person seeking selection then the choosing is done by the members voting. You may also convince the Party to place you near the top of the party list. This would increase your chances of getting into Parliament if you miss out in your electorate.

3 Now the hard work starts. You have to campaign in your electorate to convince the people that the policies that your party has are best for them and the country. How can you do it successfully? You will need to do most of the following.

- Make announcements to the news media about your policies.
- Write letters to people in your electorate.
- Go to occasions such as the opening of buildings or local markets and meet as many people as you can so they will recognise your face and name.
- Talk at public meetings about your ideas.
- Print lots of pamphlets for home delivery and have big signs made to put up around your electorate.

 ISBN 9780170182232

- Develop a web site, and if possible a social networking page, on the Internet.
- Talk to small groups.
- Call on people at home.

4 On election day hope that more people vote for you than any other candidate standing in your electorate.

5 Make sure that you still have enough votes after all the Special Votes have been counted a few days after the election. Special Votes are those votes recorded by people who are outside their electorates on polling day or who can't make it to a polling booth.

6 Under Mixed Member Proportional (MMP) voting you might still get into Parliament even if some other candidate beats you in the electorate. If you are high enough up on your party's list you could get in. MMP tries to make sure your party has the same percentage of seats in Parliament as the percentage of votes it gets.

Congratulations! You can now step into Parliament representing your political party.

Activities

1 There are six steps outlined in Resource 1. Draw a flow diagram with six boxes and linking arrows. In each box put the one or two key words from each step. Call your diagram 'Making it into Parliament'.

2 Get into groups of 3 or 4. Each group is to be a political party. Choose enough policy areas as there are members of the group. Examples are Health, Education, Defence, Agriculture/ Forestry, Police, Transport, Welfare, External Affairs. In your groups discuss and record what your party would offer the electors in each of these policy areas. Prepare a wall display for your party showing what your party would do if you were elected.

3 Politicians today use the internet to connect with possible voters. As a possible MP, design your page for a social networking site such as You Tube, Bebo or Face book.

4 Using the Net:
Make a list of 'famous firsts' in New Zealand politics. These could include the first person to be head of a New Zealand government, first person to be called 'Prime Minister', first Maori MP, first woman MP, first woman Cabinet member, first woman Prime Minister, first New Zealand born Prime Minister.

When using the internet make sure you reference the websites you visit. Do the same for any books or published material you use.

How are ideas made into laws?

You have won the right to represent your electorate in the recent elections. Your party has either most of the Members of Parliament belonging to it or your party has combined with another party to gain most Members in Parliament. Because of this your party is the government.

You now have to put into place all the ideas you supported when you were campaigning.

One of the major functions of government is to take ideas that people support and turn them into laws so that everyone behaves in a certain way for the benefit of society.

Steps by which an idea becomes a law

1 An idea comes into Parliament. This could be from the Government, the Opposition, an individual MP or interested people.

2 The idea is written up. The idea is called a Bill and writing it up is called drafting it. It is the same as when you write a draft copy of some work before you do a good copy.

3 The Bill has its first reading in Parliament. It is read by the MP who supports it. This is the first time MPs can vote for or against it.

4 The Bill is sent to a Select Committee. The committee studies it in detail. Any interested person can submit ideas on the Bill to this committee.

5 The Bill is returned to Parliament for its second reading. It is voted on again.

6 The Bill is voted on clause by clause (each part of the Bill is called a clause). This is called the 'House in Committee' stage.

7 The Bill is read to Parliament for a third time. Another vote is taken.

8 The Bill is now signed by the Governor-General and it becomes an Act of Parliament and therefore one of the laws of our society.

NOTE: If more people vote against than for the Bill in the first, second or third readings, the Bill is rejected.

 ISBN 9780170182232

This may seem a slow process. However, let's look at the strengths of the system.

- The idea is written up by people employed by Parliament and skilled in writing these documents.
- No one person can say 'This is going to be the law' and it happens.
- The idea has to be brought to the full Parliament (excluding the Governor-General) three times to make sure everyone has a chance to debate it.
- People outside Parliament have a chance to have their input in the Select Committee stage.
- The Governor-General acts as a final check. If the Governor-General is convinced that the idea is not in the best interests of our society he/she has the power to refuse to sign it. The idea would be either rejected or go back to Parliament for amendments.

Activities

1 Make a summary of Resource 1 in diagram form. Alongside the steps, show which ones you could be involved in as a private citizen, and which ones your mother could be involved in as an MP.

2 Using the Net:
Choose a current Act that has been passed in New Zealand. Briefly state what the intention of the Act is and what impact it has or may have had on New Zealanders. You can choose one from Resource 3 in Unit 13 or go onto the internet site www.legislation.govt.nz and select one.

When using the internet make sure you reference the websites you visit. Do the same for any books or published material you use.

ISBN 9780170182232

From where does government get money and how does government spending impact on me?

Governments in a modern state collect money (called taxes) from their population. In return, they provide goods and services to that population so that the state or country can run smoothly.

The idea is based on the belief that some goods and services are just too big for individual people to provide for themselves. People have not always benefited directly from paying taxes. In early Britain, for example, some people paid in produce so that they could farm a plot of land. However, they sometimes ended up with not enough to eat or were taxed by the king to fund far-away wars.

Central and local governments are not the only taxers. In some areas of the world taxes are paid to local strongmen for 'protection'. Some religious movements in the past received donations to ensure safe passage to the afterlife or for the forgiveness of misdemeanours (sins).

Where does the money come from?

2009 Estimates for the NZ Government

Source www.treasury.govt.nz

Source	Amount (in millions $)
Income tax	27,184
Corporate tax	9,028
Other income taxes	2,834
GST	11,890
Fuel	813
Tobacco	151
Customs duty	1,859
Road user charges	940
Alcohol	605
Gaming (Gambling)	254
Motor vehicle	229
Energy resources	43
ACC levies	2,780
Fire service levies	303
Earthquake / War damage levies	87

ISBN 9780170182232

And where does the money go?

NZ Government expenditure as at 30 June 2008

Source www.treasury.govt.nz

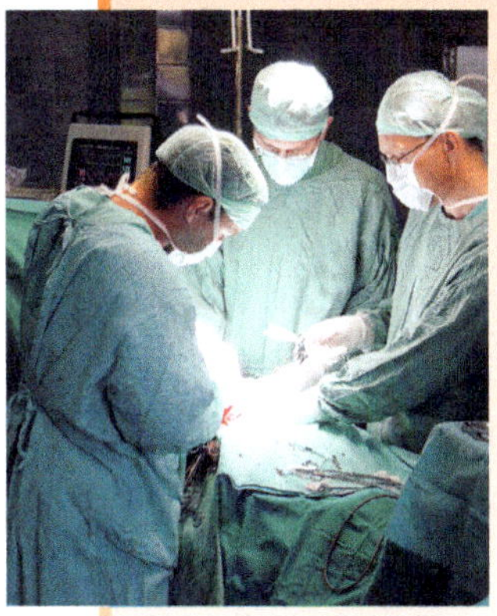

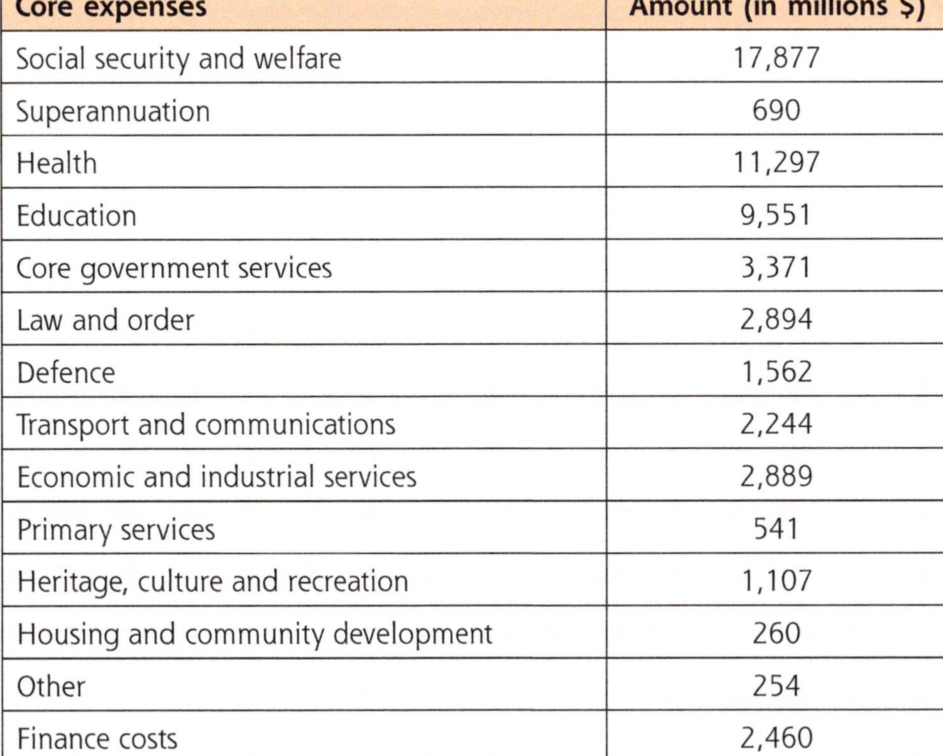

Core expenses	Amount (in millions $)
Social security and welfare	17,877
Superannuation	690
Health	11,297
Education	9,551
Core government services	3,371
Law and order	2,894
Defence	1,562
Transport and communications	2,244
Economic and industrial services	2,889
Primary services	541
Heritage, culture and recreation	1,107
Housing and community development	260
Other	254
Finance costs	2,460

Activities

1 Using Resources 1–3 design a chart displaying what your group thinks are the advantages and disadvantages of paying taxes.

2 Using Resource 2, construct a pie graph showing the six main sources of government income. Group the rest together to create the seventh segment. See if your teacher will let you use graphing software to complete this task.

3 Refer to Resource 3. Imagine you lived in a country that did not have taxes. Describe how you would go about providing six of the core services for your family.

4 Using the Net:
Find the key features of the latest government Budget.

When using the internet make sure you reference the websites you visit. Do the same for any books or published material you use.

ISBN 9780170182232

How does our type of government affect our lives?

Values are things we hold valuable, such as friendship, and people being safe from murder. Beliefs are things we hold to be true, such as democracy being better than having no government at all. These values and beliefs are often expressed as rights we think we have. You will often hear people saying that they have the right to do something or that it is their right to believe something.

However, with every right to do or believe something there is a matching responsibility that you also have.

Examples of values and beliefs

We believe ...

- that all people over a certain age should have a say in how they are governed.
- that we should be able to vote out those who govern for us if they don't do the job we want them to do.
- in the idea that people are different.
- that there is often more than one way to solve problems.
- in the idea that people can believe in different systems of government.
- that we should do what the majority of our group chooses to do.
- that anyone can put themselves forward to be chosen as a member of a government.
- that the choice we make as to who governs us is our own business.
- that all people should be able to say what they want to say.

Your individual rights

You have the right to ...

- choose a political candidate in secret.
- vote in a general election every three years.
- speak freely.
- think and act differently from others.
- vote if you are over 18.
- have your ideas accepted if the majority of people agree with you.
- support other systems of government.
- offer alternative solutions to problems.
- stand as a candidate and try to become a Member of Parliament.

 ISBN 9780170182232

Your individual responsibilities

You have the responsibility to ...

- make sure that what you say is accurate.
- represent all the people in your area if you are elected.
- accept that other people may think and act differently to you.
- vote in the general elections.
- not interfere with how other people vote.
- acknowledge that other people may believe in different ways of government.
- accept that your solution to a problem may not be the only one.
- acknowledge that others will disagree with you even if most people agree with your actions.
- register on the Electoral Roll when you turn 18.

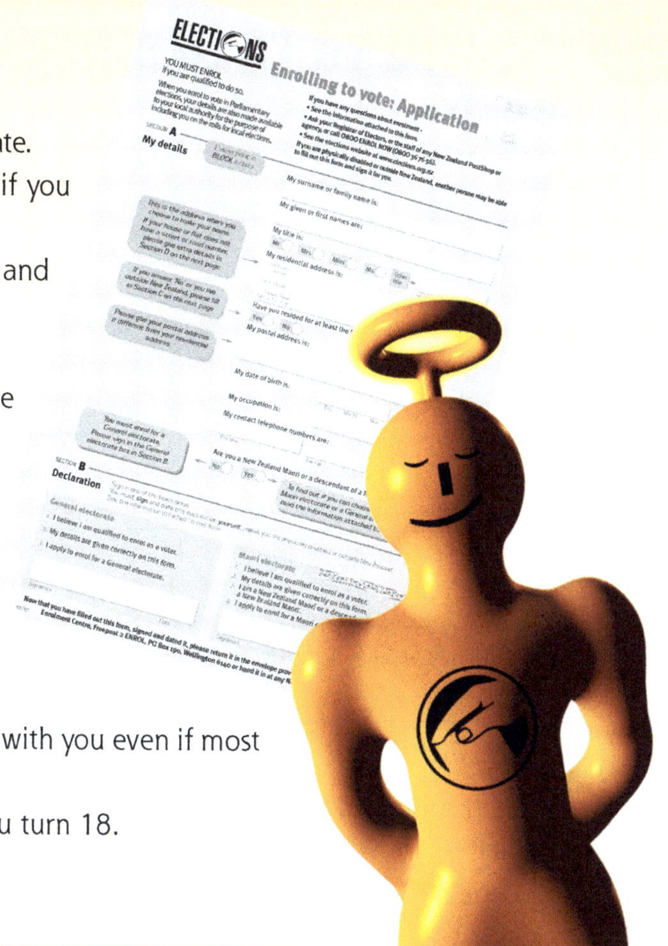

resource 2

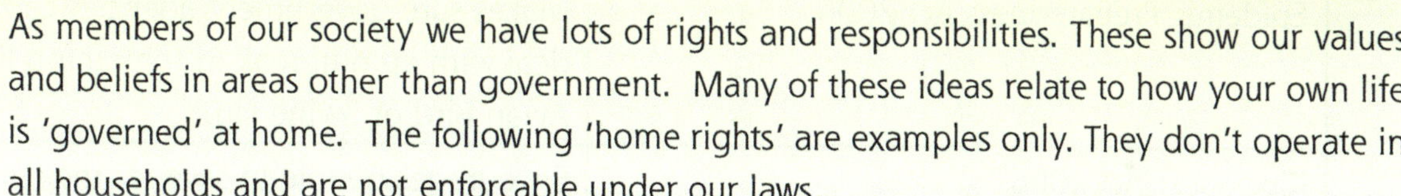

As members of our society we have lots of rights and responsibilities. These show our values and beliefs in areas other than government. Many of these ideas relate to how your own life is 'governed' at home. The following 'home rights' are examples only. They don't operate in all households and are not enforcable under our laws.

Home rights	Home responsibilities
You have the right to quiet when doing your homework.	You have the responsibility to keep quiet while others are working at home.
You have the right to food, shelter and love at home.	You have the responsibility to assist your parents wherever possible.
You have the right to times for relaxation.	You have the responsibility to ensure your relaxation activities don't intrude on others.
You have the right to your own personal space.	You have the responsibility of keeping your personal space in a manner not likely to offend other family members.

ISBN 9780170182232

Parliament passes Acts that affects all aspects of the lives of its citizens.

Act	Purpose
Affiliate Te Arawa Iwi and Hapu claims Settlement Act 2008	Records Crown settling historical Maori grievance.
Criminal Disclosures Act 2008	Sets up guidelines for the giving of information between prosecution and defence.
Real Estate Agents Act 2008	Helps the consumer buy and sell property.
Human Tissues Act 2008	Makes sure public is protected in this medical issue.
Walking Access Act 2008	Makes sure people continue to have free access to the outdoors.
Waste Minimisation Act 2008	Encourages people to cut down on rubbish.
Unsolicited Electronic Messages Act 2007	Cuts down on spam.
Immigration Advisors Licencing Act 2007	Helps people get advice about shifting from one country to another.
Epidemic Preparedness Act 2006	Makes sure government agencies can deal with an outbreak of something like Avian Bird or Swine Flu.
Kiwi Saver Act 2006	Encourages people to save for their retirement.

The Bill of Rights Act contains important rights. Everybody in government (including government departments, courts, state-owned enterprises and local authorities) must comply with the Bill of Rights Act.

The Bill of Rights Act protects you from the actions of anyone in government who interferes with your rights.

The Bill of Rights Act can protect your rights in two ways:

- The Courts can recognise your rights. However, the Courts may need to balance your rights against the rights of others and the interest of the whole community.
- The Bill of Rights requires the Attorney General to report to Parliament if any proposed law appears inconsistent with the Bill of Rights Act. The government will have to justify the need for such a law.

ISBN 9780170182232

The Act says that any limits on your rights must be reasonable.

The Bill of Rights Act contains the following rights and freedom:

1 Rights concerning fife and security of the person
2 Democratic and civil rights
3 Non-discrimination and minority rights
4 Rights concerning search, arrest, and detention
5 Rights related to criminal procedure
6 Right to justice

Activities

1 Resource 1 is deliberately mixed up. Draw up a chart like the one here and re-enter the information so that the values and beliefs, rights and responsibilities match up.

Use one colour for the values and beliefs, another colour for the corresponding rights and a third colour for the matching responsibility.

Values and beliefs	Your rights	Your responsibilities

2 Copy Resource 2. In groups see if you can establish another six rights and corresponding responsibilities that your group members have at home. Compare your findings with other groups, and take time to discuss any different rights and responsibilities you might find.

3 Refer to the club rules you wrote at in Unit 1. What rights and responsibilities did you decide the members had? Do you need to add any more in light of what you know now?

4 Produce a chart defining the following key words:

belief value right responsibility

5 Explain how each of the Acts in Resource 3 may affect you now or in the future.

6 Using the Net:
Find a copy of the New Zealand Bill of Rights. Locate at least one right you have under each of the six headings outlined in Resource 4.

When using the internet make sure you reference the websites you visit. Do the same for any books or published material you use.

ISBN 9780170182232

How do government decisions affect our lives?

The New Zealand Public Service is made up of agencies which help government frame and make up policy and put it in action. These agencies are also referred to as 'The State Sector' of our economy. Most of these agencies are answerable to a Minister of the Crown such as the Minister of Education. They are known as a Ministry, such as the Ministry of Defence, or a Department, such as the Department of Conservation.

Some just give advice to their Ministers. Some do jobs. For example, the Ministry of Social Welfare advises the Minister of Social Welfare. It also helps needy people through WINZ (Work and Income New Zealand), which is one of its divisions.

The relationship between a Ministry and its agency - Ministry of Defence and the New Zealand Defence Force.

According to the Ministry's web site The Ministry of Defence is responsible for:

- advising the government on the defence of New Zealand and its interests
- acquiring military equipment
- accessing and auditing the New Zealand Defence Force functions, duties and projects.

The New Zealand Defence Force is responsible for:

- managing the armed forces on a day-to-day basis
- delivering the government's defence policy.

Check out www.teara.govt.nz and www.wikipedia.org for additional information.

One way to find how government policy can affect your life is to look at the Government Department contacts section of your telephone directory.

The following is a summary of the Department of Internal Affairs from the 2009 Wellington phone book.

Head Office
Birth, Deaths and Marriages
Local Government and Community
Gambling Compliance Unit
Congratulatory Messages service
Ministry of Civil Defence and Emergency Management

Passports
Citizenship
Authentication Unit
Censorship Compliance Unit
Office of Ethnic Affairs
The Translation Service

ISBN 9780170182232

Activities

1 Using Resource 1 as a starter, write a paragraph describing how you think the Public Service could help government policies impact on your life.

2 You are tired of government interfering in your life. Draft a letter to your local Member of Parliament complaining about this issue. Use Resource 2 to give you some ideas!

3 Use the Government Department contacts page of your local telephone book to prepare a chart. The aim of your chart is to show how government agencies can affect your life.

4 Using the Net:
Access a Ministry web site of your choice and record what they state their main functions are. For example www.minedu.govt.nz gives you access to the Ministry of Education.

When using the internet make sure you reference the websites you visit. Do the same for any books or published material you use.

ISBN 9780170182232

unit fifteen

What other systems of government exist?

There are a range of government systems that have been tried in various places. We have already studied one, the democratic system. At the opposite end is the dictatorial system. In between is the one-party system where you have the right to vote but only for members of the same party. Russia had this system when it had a Communist Government. There are also ineffective multi-party systems where the dominant party uses its strength to make laws which weaken any opposition parties to a point where they are totally ineffective. This system only looks good on paper because there appears to be more than one party to choose from.

In the next few units we are going to examine the dictatorial system. We will use Germany as our case study because this nation, under a dictatorial system, had such an effect on world events last century. We will also briefly look at how Russia changed from a one-party state to a democracy.

A case study of how people changed from a dictatorial system to a democracy – The Russian Federation.

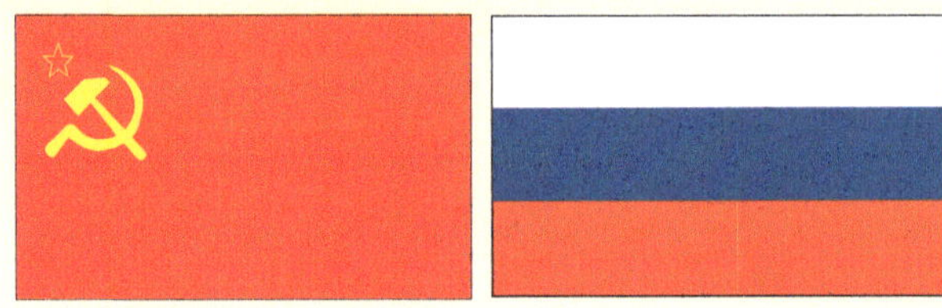

The USSR used to be one of two super-powers of the world. The other was the United States of America. USSR stood for Union of Soviet Socialist Republics. It was made up of the Russian republic under a communist government and 14 border republics which were controlled by Russia.

The Communist Party was the only political party allowed in the USSR and it was controlled by one leader. The party was in charge of every aspect of life. It operated from Moscow, the capital of Russia. If you publicly disagreed with the party you could be jailed or even killed.

In 1985 Mikhail Gorbachev became the new leader. He started to <u>restructure</u> so that less was spent on weapons and more on agriculture. He allowed <u>people to have more say</u> on the farms and in the factories where they worked, particularly on how they could improve the running of these businesses.

He also <u>encouraged an openness</u> in Soviet society. This meant people could say what they really thought.

Under Gorbachev's leadership the 15 republics <u>held free elections</u>. Many non-communists were elected. Many of the border republics declared their independence from the Soviet Union.

In August 1991 some of the people who were losing power in Russia staged a military coup to restore power to the Communist Party. They <u>did not have the support of the armed forces</u> and the coup failed.

ISBN 9780170182232

In December 1991 the 15 republics agreed to end the Soviet Union. Eleven of them chose to form the Russian Federation. Since then Russia has struggled to build a democratic political system and market economy to replace the strict social, political and economic controls of the communist period. Russia changed from a one-party state to a democracy.

Characteristics of different types of governments

Some types	Characteristics of some governments
• Absolute Monarchy • Autocracy • Democracy • Federation • Military Dictatorship • Monarchy • Republic • Theocracy	• Political power is held by representatives who are elected by the people who are represented. • Political power is held by a single person, often called a President (or dictator by their opponents!). • Kings or Queens (King or queen rules) ruling the country, usually with appointed advisors. • The military holds all political power with the Head of the Military being Head of State. • A group of people, representing a particular religion, holds all political power. • A central government shares power with a number of smaller, local governments. • A government where a president is the Head of State and has decision-making powers. • A King or Queen is Head of State but is more of a figure head. Government is led by an elected Prime Minister who works with a Parliament elected by the people.

One issue that has interested New Zealanders is whether or not New Zealand should be a republic. A republic does not have a member of a royal family, such as Queen Elizabeth 11, as its head of state. Instead it usually has a home-grown President.

You are a member of the Constitutional Review Select Committee. A bill has been introduced into Parliament declaring New Zealand to be a republic and therefore removing the Queen as our Head of State. Your committee's task is to hear all the submissions.

1. It is time we stopped thinking of ourselves as a colony and grew up. Our Head of State should be one of us.
2. We don't need a president. We already have an effective Head of State in the Governor-General who represents the Queen.
3. Our English heritage is as important to us as our non-English heritage. There is no advantage to us to declare ourselves a republic.
4. History is for the old people. It is time we moved on and joined the rest of the world in the 21st century.
5. The Queen of England and her family are not relevant to modern New Zealanders. They live half a world away. We need to focus on our area of the Pacific.

ISBN 9780170182232

6 We are an immigrant nation. Having a Queen gives us all something in common.

7 We are already cutting ties with Great Britain. We no longer have access to the Privy Council as the highest court and nothing terrible has happened to us as a nation.

8 It is good to have a Head of State who is not influenced by the day-to-day politicians of a country. The Queen provides that.

9 I'm a second generation New Zealander with an Italian heritage. What has the Queen of England got to do with me and all the other New Zealanders who don't have English ancestors?

10 The Americans are always searching for a replacement to royalty. Look at the way they treat their President and First Lady! We already have access to royalty, why throw it away?

11 In 1840 we signed a treaty with the Queen of England. If we replace her descendants with some other Head of State we will lose one half of the treaty partners. This is not good for our country!

12 If we became a republic we could no longer have the prefix "Royal" for our Navy, Air force and Corps within the NZ Army. Men and women died defending our way of life under those banners. Becoming a republic is disrespectful of their sacrifice.

13 The Governor–Generals, as the Queen's representatives, are already chosen by the Government. Why can't they be our Head of State in a republic?

14 A republic? No way. Do you want New Zealand to end up like Zimbabwe or even Fiji?

Activities

1 Draw a line across your page like the one below. This is called a continuum. At one end place the word 'Democracy', and at the other end place the word 'Dictatorship'. Along your continuum put the other two systems mentioned in the first paragraph of this unit. Head up your continuum 'Some systems of government'.

Continuum

Dictatorship ——————————————— **Democracy**

2 Using Resource 1 write between 50 and 100 words showing how people changed the dictatorship of the Communist Party to a democracy. To help you, the key points are underlined. Illustrate your work with the old and new flags of Russia.

3 Using the information in Resource 2 draw up a three-column chart and match the type of government with its corresponding characteristics. The third column can be filled in once you have completed the research activity below.

4 Using the Net:
Locate two countries of each of type of government and add them to your chart in Activity 3.

When using the internet make sure you reference the websites you visit. Do the same for any books or published material you use.

ISBN 9780170182232

How did the Nazi Party rise to power in Germany?

Most dictators arise when there are extreme conditions. For example, there may be extremes of wealth and poverty, there may be extreme economic hardship or there may be extreme religious feelings or nationalistic (thinking your country is the best and being willing to do anything for it) feelings. In 1929 the Great Depression spread around the world. Depression hit hard at Germany. Many people were thrown out of work. Living standards dropped. Germans started to experience extreme economic hardship. The Nazi Party under the leadership of Adolf Hitler grew in strength. Hitler offered jobs and a belief that Germany would once again become the great nation it had been before it lost World War 1.

The Nazi Party used the feelings of despair created by extreme economic hardship to get votes. It held rallies and speeches to encourage nationalistic feelings.

By 1932 the Nazi Party had won enough seats in the German Parliament to join with other smaller parties to become the government. Hitler became Prime Minister.

For the next year the Nazi Party promised all things to all groups. To big business it promised contracts for weapons, and to crush trade unions. To the armed forces it promised expansion and new weapons. To the workers it promised jobs. To all people it promised law and order and an end to street battles.

In 1933 there was another election. This time the Nazi Party won enough seats to be the government by itself. As Prime Minister, Hitler passed a law that banned all political opposition. Thus Germany moved from a democratic system of government to a dictatorial system (dictatorship). Hitler, as Head of State of a one-party government, could come to be regarded as a dictator.

Activities

1 Draw up a simple flow diagram (about 4 boxes) and show how the Nazi Party came to power. Head up your flow diagram 'From Democracy to Dictatorship'.

2 Construct a Nazi Party election poster which would encourage people to vote for that party.

3 Using the Net:
'The depression put wind into Hitler's sails.'
Find some evidence to back up this famous quote.

When using the internet make sure you reference the websites you visit. Do the same for any books or published material you use.

ISBN 9780170182232

How did the Nazi Party control German society?

As a dictator, your objective is to control every part of society. The Nazi Party set up a system of control based on geographic regions. At the top of the system was Adolf Hitler. At the bottom were the block wardens.

In between were four groups of people, each group responsible for a larger area than the group below them.

Nazi Party policy ideas started with Hitler and his advisors. The ideas were handed down the chain of command until block wardens told people what they, the people, were responsible for.

Anyone who didn't carry out the orders of the block warden could be reported to the regular police force or the secret police force (the Gestapo).

Control of education

By controlling what young people were taught, the Nazi Party could control what they learnt. Through the education system children were taught that some Germans were superior to others and that Germany had a glorious history based on military successes.

Children were also taught that it was their duty to report on their parents and teachers if these people said anything against the Nazi Party. In this way Nazi ideas could be taken right into the home. Duty and loyalty to Germany was more important than duty and loyalty to the family.

Some of the ideas taught in various subject areas were:

READING:	Glorious battle stories were introduced to replace the more traditional stories about animals and people.
MATHEMATICS:	Geometry became the study of curves and angles related to shell and bomb paths (the study of ballistics).
HISTORY:	Emphasis was placed on German military successes throughout history and especially before World War One when Germany had an empire.
SOCIAL STUDIES:	Emphasis was on the qualities and successes of the light-skinned races of which Germans were said to be the best. This is where the idea of a 'master race' was taught. Anyone who did not fit into the category of light-skin and master-race was said to be inferior.
BIOLOGY:	Racial lessons were taught which re-emphasised the lessons learnt in Social Studies.

 ISBN 9780170182232

Control of youth groups

The Nazis increased government influence over young people. They closed down traditional youth groups like Scouting and Guiding. They made all 10 to 18 year olds join a branch of the Hitler Youth Movement.

In many ways the Hitler Youth Movement was like Scouting and Guiding. Camps were arranged where bushcraft and camp-craft skills were taught. There were lots of fun activities, trips away, sports and games. Gymnastics and cross-country running were also popular. However, there was more to the movement's aims than just having fun. Both boys and girls were taught parade ground skills to develop their self-discipline and their nationalistic feelings. For the boys, this meant that they would fit comfortably into a military unit when they were over 18. Girls were taught home-making skills such as how to look after young ones, sewing and cooking. This was intended to make them want to be good German mothers.

Throughout their time in the Hitler Youth Movement young people were fed a steady diet of films and lectures on how good the Nazi Party was and how it was doing great things for Germany. No one was allowed to criticise what was going on and anyone who tried to leave was punished.

Hitler Youth members

ISBN 9780170182232

Control of the news media

To make sure your ideas are the only ones people are allowed to hear you have to control what is being said so that people will believe only what you tell them.

To do that you have to set up a system which controls what people read, see and hear. These systems of control are called 'censorship'.

The following news media were controlled:

NEWSPAPERS:	Editors were told what to print and how to say things so that articles always supported the Nazi Government.
RADIO:	This was a good way for all Germans to listen at the same time to Hitler. The Nazis could also block foreign or anti-Nazi broadcasts.
FILMS:	Germany had an active film industry. Film makers were controlled so that only films showing the glories of Germany and how well the Nazi Government was doing were allowed to be made.
BOOKS:	Any book that was considered to be anti-German was either banned or burnt. Prior to 1939 there were huge book burning events in many German universities.
FOREIGN PUBLICATIONS AND FILMS:	To ensure that the German people only saw, read and heard what the Nazi Government wanted them to, all foreign publications and films had to be approved by a government official. This made sure that the German people would not find out about how other people viewed the events in Germany.

Effects of Nazi Government policy on German people's lives

By 1937-38 most Germans felt things were 'looking up' under a Nazi Party Government.

- Labour unions were banned so unrest in the general work force was reduced.
- Huge public works programmes were started which provided jobs. The development of Germany's autobahns (motorways) is an example.
- Industry expanded to produce war materials such as new tanks, artillery, aircraft and ships.
- Money was spent on the scientific community, particularly research and development of weapons.
- Improved consumer products began reaching the general public. The development of the Volkswagen, the people's car, is an example although the Second World War slowed its production.
- Banking was regulated and inflation brought under control.
- The Nazi Government refused to pay any more money to the World War 1 Allies as demanded under the Treaty of Versailles (made at the end of World War 1 which Germany lost) and ignored restrictions on Germany's Armed Forces (which the Allies demanded).

ISBN 9780170182232

Activities

1 Draw a plan of your classroom.
- Divide your room in half. Give each half a regional name.
- Now divide each region into two sub-regions.
- Now divide each sub-region into two blocks. (There should be eight blocks on your plan.)
- Now draw 3-4 desks in each block.
- Label one desk in each block the 'Block Warden'.
- Label one desk in each sub-region the 'Cell Warden'.
- Label one desk in each region 'Regional Warden'.
- Add another desk into the room and label it 'Dictator'.
- Draw lines of communication from the Dictator through the wardens to the people in each block.
- Colour code your desks and remember to use a key.

Write a brief description of how an idea would get from the Dictator to the people.

2 It is 1938. You are a German school student of your own age with a pen-pal in New Zealand. Use Resources 2 and 6 to help you write a letter to your pen-pal describing what changes you are experiencing in your schooling. Share your ideas with other group members before starting your good copy.

3 Make up a cartoon strip of a German child trying to convince his or her parents to let him or her join the Hitler Youth Movement.

4 Using the Net:
Complete one of the following research activities.
- Little is commonly known about life for children of your age in war-time Germany. In your group search for knowledge and construct a presentation on what you discover.
- An infamous dictator from the early 21st century is Robert Mugabe. Find out the effect of his government on the people of Zimbabwe.

When using the internet make sure you reference the websites you visit. Do the same for any books or published material you use.

What happened if you opposed Nazi ideas?

There were two major groups in German society who were treated harshly. The first were those who believed in other political ideas or behaved in a way that the Nazi Government classified as anti-German. A lot of politicians, church priests, teachers and other educated members of German society were included in this category. These people were gathered up and sent to special camps where they were 're-educated'.

If you resisted re-education you were put in a concentration camp and worked as slave labour until you died. There was no such thing as a right to a fair trial following your arrest.

The other group was the large Jewish population. These people were as German as their non-Jewish neighbours but they were targeted by the Nazi Government as people to blame for all Germany's problems.

Boycotts of Jewish businesses were followed by the destruction of Jewish property. By 1942 the Nazi Government had decided to kill the entire Jewish population of Europe. Gas chambers were set up in concentration camps and over 6 million Jewish men, women and children were put to death.

Rachel's diary December 1944

Today the government official came to our home and told us to prepare to move. We are to be taken from our home where my mother was born and our house is now owned by the government. We have not been paid for it. He said that we are going to a new settlement in the east.

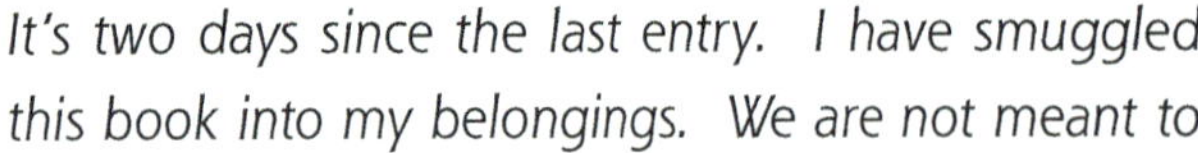

It's two days since the last entry. I have smuggled this book into my belongings. We are not meant to write anything. The night before last the whole family was dragged out of bed at 2am and ordered onto a fleet of trucks parked in the street. I could see our Jewish neighbours three houses away being loaded as well. We had no time to dress warmly but luckily we took seriously the official's warning to prepare and we already had our small bags packed with essential clothing. We were taken to the railway station and loaded into cattle carriages. They stank!

We left the city only to be placed on a railway siding for a day where we stayed and did nothing. No one was allowed out and the door had to be kept closed. I crawled up to a small vent in the wall and could see fields outside and get a breath of air. We have had nothing to eat or drink.

 ISBN 9780170182232

We have been on this train 5 days now and every day at least one person in our carriage dies. Once a day the guards open the door and we have to pass out the dead. We are given bread and water. It is bitterly cold as we go east into the winter.

This morning was terrible. The train came to a halt just after 9am and the guards ordered everyone out. We had to line up on this platform in the freezing weather and then move slowly to a table where an officer sat. My watch was taken so I don't know the time anymore. Beyond the station I could see barbed wire fences and buildings with tall chimneys. Worst of all I was separated from my parents and little brother. The officer just nodded at me and I was dragged one way while the rest of my family went the other way. I am now lying on a wooden bunk in a long barrack room with one thin blanket and the clothes I came in with. I am going to hide this book because I think tomorrow I am going to lose all my clothes and be given a terrible garment to wear. It also looks like I am going to have my head shaved.

ISBN 9780170182232

Concentration camp conditions

Daily Routine

Summer

0400 hrs	Get up
0515 hrs	Roll call
0545-0600 hrs	Breakfast
0600-1200 hrs	Work
1200-1300 hrs	Dinner
1300-1830 hrs	Work
1900 hrs	Roll call (1 hour)
2000-2045 hrs	Meal time
2045 hrs	Barracks
2100 hrs	Lights out

Winter

0500 hrs	Get up
Dawn till dusk	Working time

Work done

- Road building
- Camp expansion programmes
- Camp duties
- Making munitions and rifles
- Working in the underground aircraft factories

Rations

Morning	350 grams bread	
	½ lt of substitute coffee	
Midday	6 times a week	– 1 lt of turnip or cabbage soup
	Once a week	– 1 lt of noodle soup
Evening	4 times a week	– 20-30 grams sausage or cheese
		– ¾ lt substitute tea
	3 times a week	– 1 lt of soup

Medical experiments

Prisoners were used for medical experiments such as:

- finding the lowest temperature humans can stand before freezing to death.
- effects of high altitude on humans without oxygen.
- injection of infectious diseases to observe and record the effects on humans.

Types of penalties

8 days detention and 25 whip strokes before and after detention:

- if you make jeering comments about the SS.
- if you forget to salute the guard properly.

 ISBN 9780170182232

14 days detention:

- if you leave or enter a building by any means other than the doors.
- if you smoke inside.

14 days detention and 25 whip strokes before and after detention:

- if you write unfavourable remarks about the Nazi Government.
- for keeping tools in the sleeping quarters.

42 days solitary confinement:

- if you insult the emblems of the Nazi state or those who wear them.

Death by hanging:

- if you try to encourage others to resist or if you send out information about camp conditions.

Punishments could consist of deprival of food, standing for many hours on the parade ground, extra work details, punishment drills, beatings, solitary confinement, suspension by wrists from a tree or pole, beating to death, hanging and shooting.

Activities

1 Rachel survived her experiences in the concentration camp and was released by Allied Forces in mid 1945. In co-operation with your group write entries in her diary outlining what you think she went through and her thoughts on her release. Illustrate your entries with a barbed wire border. You may like to use the information in Resource 3, or alternatively do some library research for additional information.

2 Using the Net:
Find out why the Nazis, and Hitler especially, hated the Jews.

When using the internet make sure you reference the websites you visit. Do the same for any books or published material you use.

ISBN 9780170182232

Could there be a dictatorship in New Zealand?

Germany was a democracy and the Nazi Party was a political party that became the government because enough people voted for it. Once in power the Nazi Party changed the system to ban all opposition. Thus Germany was ruled by a dictatorship.

The Nazi Party followed a foreign policy which eventually helped to cause World War 2. It took the total military defeat of Germany in 1945 to allow democracy to be re-established. Could a dictator become established in New Zealand?

We have a democracy. So did Germany. We have a system of government that allows the party with the most people in Parliament to form the government. So did Germany. What is there to stop a party becoming the government and then changing the rules in New Zealand?

The answer lies in your hands because most of you have, or will have, the right to vote. One of the purposes of the comparison you have just studied is to make you aware of how a democracy became a dictatorship. This knowledge is what will prevent a dictatorial system being set up here. You will be able to recognise the signs and thus preserve the democratic system of social control we enjoy in New Zealand.

Activities

1 Your group is to plan a publicity campaign which will explain to New Zealanders why they must preserve the democratic system of government.

Some suggestions:

- Design and write a pamphlet to be dropped in mail boxes.
- Design and make publicity posters.
- Plan, write and record (using a tape recorder) a 30 second radio advertisement.

2 Using the Net:

Create a website to accompany the above activity.

When using the internet make sure you reference the websites you visit. Do the same for any books or published material you use.

ISBN 9780170182232

Glossary of political terms

Act of Parliament A law passed by Parliament.
Amendments Changes sought to original documents.
Backbenchers Members of the government not in Cabinet.
Ballot Box The box into which you place your completed voting paper.
Ballot paper The form on which you record your choices in an election.
Belief Accepting as true.
Benefits Those things offered by membership of a particular group
Bill An idea for a possible law that has been drafted and presented to Parliament.
Cabinet Senior members of the government with responsibilities to look after government departments.
Candidate A person standing for Parliament who seeks your vote.
Casting a vote The process of voting.
Caucus A meeting of all the Members of Parliament from a particular political party.
Civil Service/ Public Service The group of people in a country employed by the government to enact and administer government decisions. The term is used to differentiate between Military and Civil services
Citizen Member of a society.
Coalition The agreement of two or more political parties to co-operate for a particular purpose.
Colony An area whose administration and law making functions are controlled by another country.
Constitution A body of fundamental principles according to which a State or other organisation is governed.
Communism A system of society with vesting of property in the community, each member working for the common benefit according to his capacity and receiving according to his needs.
Coup An illegal change of government.
Democracy A form of government in which the people's wishes are carried out by a Parliament elected by the people.
Dictatorship A form of parliament where one person or party holds absolute power.
Elect The process of choosing from a range of people.
Elected MP A Member of Parliament who is elected to represent an electorate (compare with 'List MP').
Electoral Roll The list of those people who are eligible to vote in an election.
Electorate The people in a particular geographic area who can vote for a Member of Parliament.
Executive Carrying out the law.
Executive Council The Governor-General and Cabinet.
General Election The selection, by voting, of all Members of Parliament.
Government The political party (or parties) which controls the public affairs of the nation.
Governor-General The Queen's representative as our Head of State.
Hapu Maori sub-tribe.

House Refers to the House of Representatives where the business of government is carried out.

Immigrant Person who shifts from one country or place to another.

Iwi Maori tribe.

Judiciary The judges and law courts that interpret the laws of the land.

Laws Formalised rules by which we control society.

Legislative Making laws.

List MP A Member of Parliament chosen from a political party's list (compare with 'Elected MP').

Local government Government at the local level, often referred to as Regional, District or City Councils.

Marae Traditional meeting place for whanau, hapu and iwi members, usually with a meeting house and dining house.

Member Refers to anyone who is a Member of Parliament.

Minister of the Crown Minister in government where Head of State is a monarch.

Ministers Senior members of government who are in Cabinet.

MMP Mixed Member Proportional representation in Parliament.

National government Government for the whole nation – not to be confused with the National Party.

Nationalism Patriotic feeling, principles or effort towards your own country.

Opposition Those Members of Parliament who are not part of the Government.

Parliament The Governor-General and all Members of Parliament elected to represent the people.

Paramount Chief Highest ranking chief.

Party List The list of all candidates of a political party from which Members of Parliament who are not directly elected are drawn depending on the proportion of the total vote that party receives in an election.

Policies The activities of government or society which political parties regard as important and which they promote.

Political Party A group of people who believe in similar policies.

Politician A person who stands for election to represent the people in Parliament.

Polling Booth A place where you go to vote in an election.

Portfolio The specific duties and responsibilities of a Minister.

Privileges Those things granted by behaving in a particular way.

Renaissance The period in European history that experienced a revival in the Arts, Science and Literature during the 14th-16th centuries.

Republic Government whose Head of State is not a monarch but (usually) a president.

Responsibility Liable to be called to account over given actions.

Right Idea of that which is due to a person or group.

Select Committee Special committees set up by Parliament to study proposed new laws.

Senate Assembly that has debating or legislative powers.

Senator Member of Senate.

Society The word given to a group of people who share common customs and organisations.

Sovereignty Supreme authority with the right to enact laws over a given area or political state.

Speaker The person who controls the debates and activities within the House of Representatives.

Special vote A vote cast by someone outside their own electorate.

State sector All organisations that report to the Crown.

Taxes Money paid by members of a population to an organisation for the provision of services to that population.

Value What one thinks to be correct and a guide for life.

Whanau Maori for family.

Writ Legal document issued by a court or judiciary officer.

ISBN 9780170182232